Everyday Heroes

E.R. Doctors

<u>Jill C. Wheeler</u>
ABDO Publishing Company

visit us at
www.abdopub.com

Published by ABDO Publishing Company, 4940 Viking Drive, Edina, Minnesota 55435.
Copyright © 2003 by Abdo Consulting Group, Inc. International copyrights reserved in all
countries. No part of this book may be reproduced in any form without written permission from
the publisher.

Printed in the United States.

Editors: Kate A. Conley, Stephanie Hedlund, Kristianne E. Vieregger
Photo Credits: Corbis
Art Direction: Neil Klinepier

Library of Congress Cataloging-in-Publication Data

Wheeler, Jill C., 1964-
 E.R. doctors / Jill C. Wheeler.
  p. cm. -- (Everyday heroes)
 Includes index.
 Summary: Discusses emergency medicine and the work of the medical personnel who
practice it.
 Contents: The golden hour -- A new type of medicine -- Life in the E.R. -- The road to
the E.R. -- The ABCs of trauma -- Inside the E.R. -- Help from technology -- The E.R.:
when to go.
 ISBN 1-57765-859-0

 1. Emergency medicine--Juvenile literature. 2. Emergency physicians--Juvenile
literature. [1. Emergency medicine. 2. Emergency physicians.] I. Title. II. Everyday
heroes (Edina, Minn.)

RC86.5 .W448
616.02'5--dc21

                                                                    2002066664

Contents

E.R. Doctors

There are many types of doctors who work to help people in different ways. They attend many years of school to learn specific types of medicine. They may learn how to perform surgery or treat diseases. But did you know there are doctors who **specialize** in emergencies?

E.R. doctors continue to learn new skills while they work.

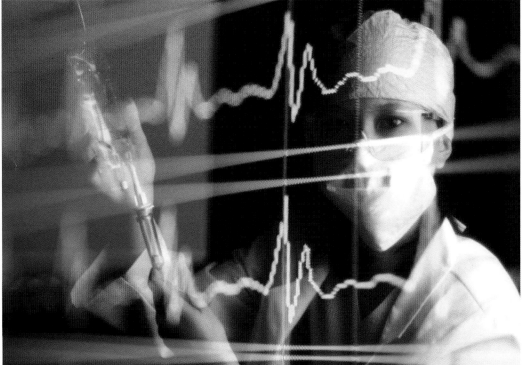

Emergency room (E.R.) doctors are a part of emergency and rescue services. E.R. doctors and nurses work with firefighters, police officers, and **Emergency Medical Technicians (EMTs)**. Like those professionals, E.R. doctors work to save lives.

E.R. doctors treat all kinds of patients. Some people come to the E.R. with colds or flus. Others come with sprains or cuts. Still others arrive at the E.R. because of more serious conditions.

E.R. doctors train for many years. They use a variety of equipment. And they continue learning throughout their career. So they are able to help anyone that comes to the E.R.

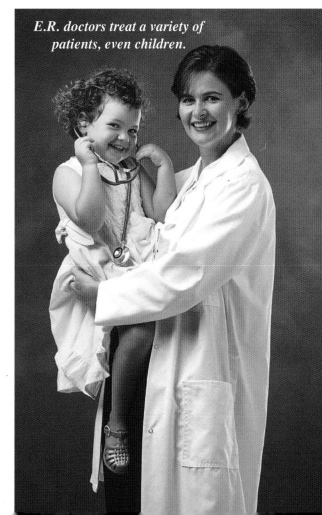

E.R. doctors treat a variety of patients, even children.

A New Type of Care

Emergency medicine is fairly new. In the early days of the United States, there were no E.R.s. Injured people had two choices. They could send for a doctor to come and see them. Or, they could go to the doctor's home or office to receive treatment.

The first horse-drawn **ambulances** appeared in the 1860s. Sometimes a doctor rode on the ambulance. However, there usually was not much he could do to help.

Emergency care improved during **World War II**. Doctors learned how to use blood **transfusions** to avoid **shock**. And they began using **antibiotics**.

By the **Korean War**, **mobile** U.S. Army hospitals appeared. These hospitals were near the battlefields. The doctors at these

Emergency medicine at the site of a battle

hospitals used a special system, called triage. The word *triage* means to sort out. Army doctors worked on the sickest patients first. Meanwhile, less critically injured patients waited for help.

By the early 1960s, emergency medicine for soldiers was well developed. But for U.S. **civilians**, there was no emergency medicine. **Ambulances** didn't carry medical assistance. Hospitals were poorly prepared to deal with emergencies. And most doctors didn't **specialize** in emergency procedures.

This horse-drawn carriage transported sick or injured people to a doctor.

That soon began to change. A small group of doctors recognized the need for **specialized** E.R. doctors. They came up with a plan to make it happen. By the early 1970s, several medical schools trained doctors in emergency medicine.

The U.S. government also helped. The government passed the Emergency Medical Services Systems Act. This led to better-equipped **ambulances**. It also developed a system to staff the ambulances with trained **EMTs**.

Today, local or state governments run most Emergency Medical Services. E.R.s are usually part of a hospital. These hospitals may be public or private. Many large E.R.s have ties to medical schools. This allows students to learn firsthand about emergency medicine.

People who are treated at an E.R. are billed by the hospital. The hospital uses part of the money to pay its E.R. staff members. Sometimes patients can't afford medical help. The doctors and nurses treat them anyway. Then the government helps pay the patients' bills.

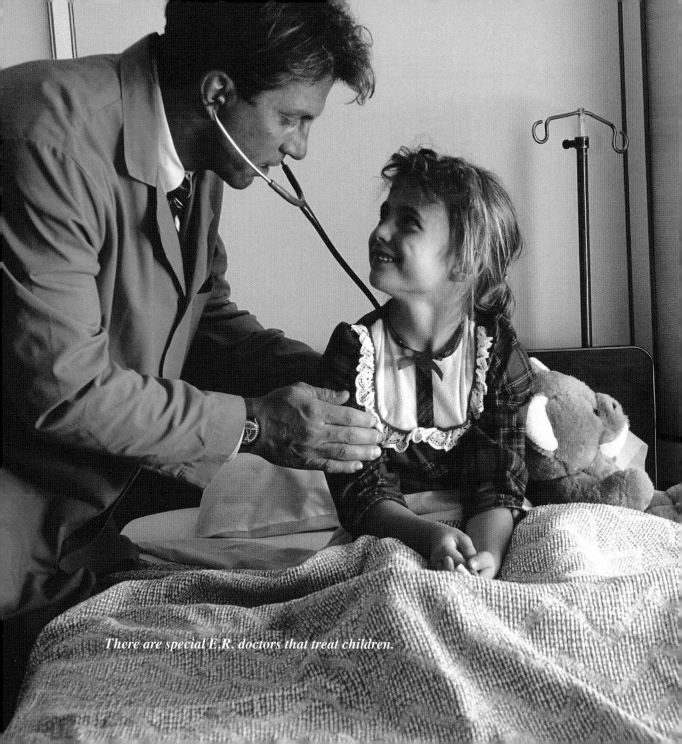

There are special E.R. doctors that treat children.

Life in the E.R.

E.R. doctors are much like other doctors. They are licensed by the state where they practice medicine. Their job is to save and prolong life.

E.R. doctors have many different duties. Not everyone who comes to the E.R. is having an emergency. E.R. doctors never know what types of cases they will see. So they must have a broad medical knowledge.

E.R. staff members take each patient's temperature and blood pressure. They listen to each patient's heart and check his or her pulse. Then they ask questions to find out what is wrong. E.R. doctors can **prescribe** medicines and refer patients to **specialists**.

People visit the E.R. if they are seriously ill or injured.

E.R. doctors work in special surroundings. The E.R. is usually the emergency medical department of a hospital. People do not make appointments to come to the E.R. So E.R. doctors may have to make someone wait if a more critically injured patient comes in. Nonemergency patients may wait for a long time to see a doctor.

E.R. doctors work quickly to give a critically injured patient the best care possible.

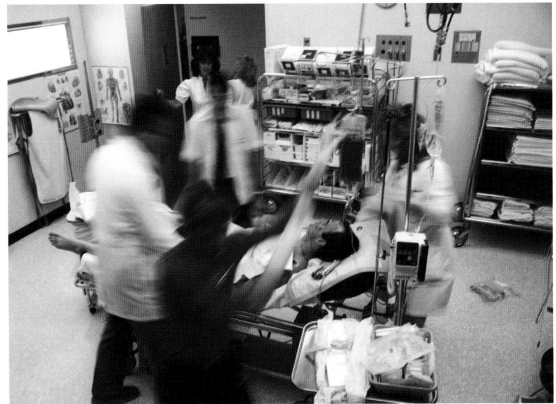

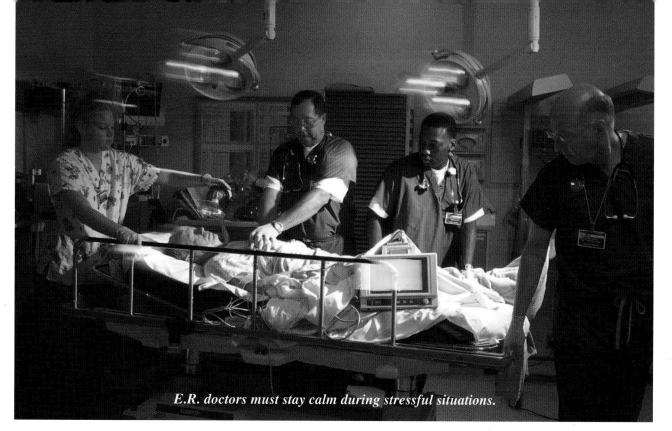

E.R. doctors must stay calm during stressful situations.

Work in an E.R. can be hectic or slow. The E.R. can be empty one minute and packed the next. E.R. doctors face many stressful events. They are under pressure to be fast yet precise. There is always the chance that they will make a mistake while treating someone.

Emergency medicine also has many rewards. E.R. doctors see more conditions than any other **specialist**. This gives them the opportunity to touch and save many lives.

The Road to the E.R.

Many E.R. doctors say they feel called to emergency medicine. They love the excitement. But they stay calm and clearheaded in the middle of extreme **chaos**.

E.R. doctors must be able to make lightning-quick decisions with certainty. They must be familiar with a wide variety of medical conditions. And they have to work well as part of a team.

To become a doctor, students must be educated for about 12 years. First, they attend four years of college. Then, they attend medical school for another

These students are learning about different types of medicines.

four years. Next, they have a year-long **internship** followed by a three-year **residency**.

In medical school, students spend their first two years in the classroom, the laboratory, and the library. They learn about the human body and clinical medicine.

During their third year of medical school, students begin to spend time around doctors and patients. This gives them a chance to see many different **specialties**. These include areas such as surgery, **pediatrics**, or emergency medicine. Meanwhile, students continue to study about medicine.

During their fourth year of medical school, students spend more time in their chosen specialty. Students who want to be E.R. doctors work in the

Students must train for a long time before they can understand all medical tests.

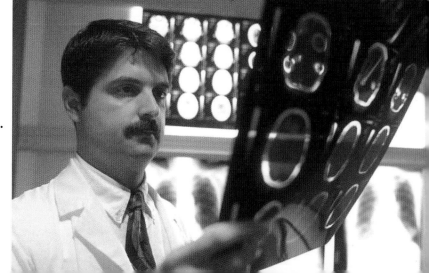

emergency medicine department. At the end of the year, they must pass tests to graduate from medical school.

Medical school graduates become **interns** for one year. Medical interns receive extra training in a hospital. They work long hours doing basic medical work. They leave the more complex jobs to experienced doctors.

E.R. doctors help each other to make sure they are giving the best care possible.

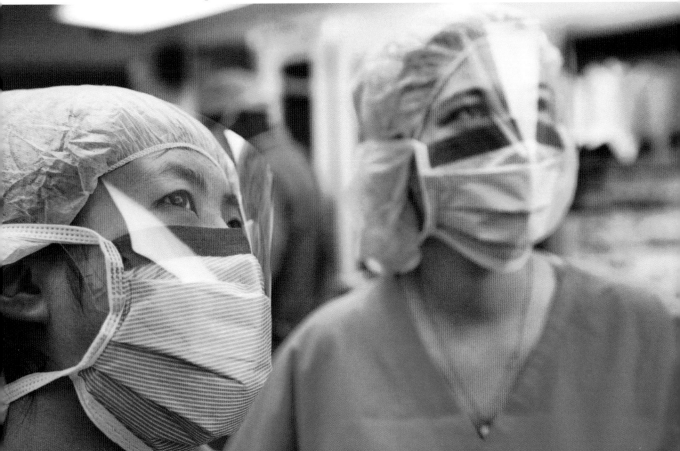

After their **internship**, students become **residents**. In emergency medicine, students are residents for about three years. They attend conferences each week. These conferences review what has happened in the department and help residents learn. After the residency, students must pass a certification exam.

Now these residents become true E.R. doctors. They can take jobs outside the teaching hospital. Or, they can stay at the teaching hospital. All doctors continue learning. They must continue their education to retain their medical licenses. E.R. doctors are no different.

ABCs of Life Support

E.R. doctors treat all kinds of problems. But they are best known for handling emergencies. Some of the most common emergencies in the United States are poisonings, heart attacks, **asthma** attacks, and assaults.

Most serious emergencies come to the E.R. by **ambulance**. By the time patients arrive, **EMTs** have already worked to stabilize them. EMTs have also called the E.R. They tell the doctors and nurses what to expect so everything can be ready.

If the patient is critically injured, a **trauma** team will be waiting when the ambulance arrives. The trauma team is dressed in gowns, gloves, and masks.

There are several members in a trauma team. Typical members are trauma surgeons, nurses, a radiologist, and a radiologist technician. There also are lab technicians to do blood work and other tests.

First, E.R. staff members determine the patient's condition. They use the ABCs of life support to do this. The letter *A* stands for airway. Doctors first check to see if anything is blocking the patient's airway.

This patient is getting help breathing with a respiration bag.

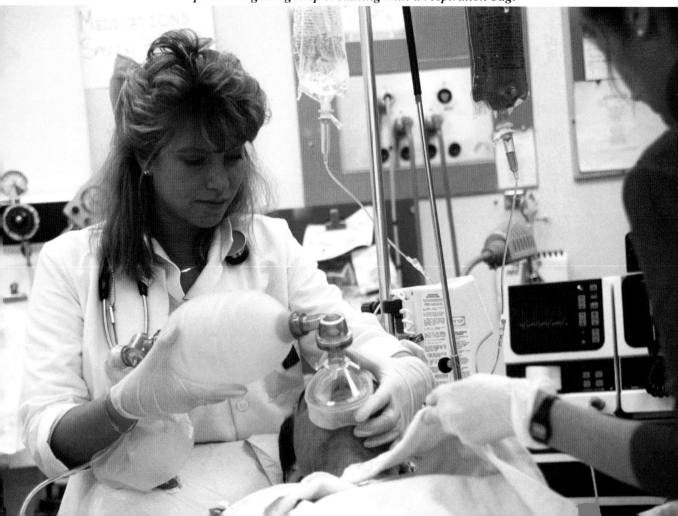

The letter *B* stands for breathing. Doctors check to see that the patient's lungs are working. If not, they may have to breathe for the patient. This is called **cardiopulmonary resuscitation**.

The letter *C* stands for circulation. Doctors and nurses make sure the patient's blood can carry oxygen throughout the body. This can't happen if the patient is bleeding heavily. **Trauma** team members put pressure on the wound to stop the bleeding.

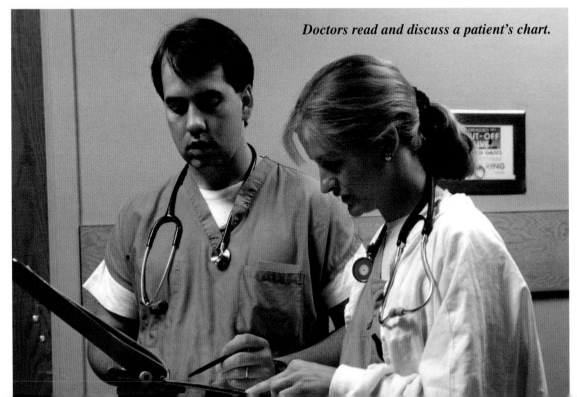

Doctors read and discuss a patient's chart.

Sometimes, doctors must do tests to find out what is wrong. Blood work, X rays, and other tests can help identify problems. E.R. doctors and nurses will ask questions to get information about the patient's condition.

Once a patient is stabilized, E.R. doctors decide where they must go next. Patients in critical condition may be sent to the hospital's intensive care unit. Other patients could be sent to surgery. If the injury is minor, the patient might be released and sent home.

Regardless of what happens, E.R. teams keep detailed records of everything that was done. This helps them constantly improve their quality of care. Police officers may also use these records. E.R. staff members routinely cooperate with other emergency workers to help their community.

Inside the E.R.

E.R.s vary greatly. Some may be quiet and small, such as in rural community hospitals. There may be just one nurse on duty at all times. Small E.R.s provide basic medical care. They can send badly injured people to larger E.R.s or **trauma** centers.

E.R. doctors, nurses, and technicians work as a team to save lives!

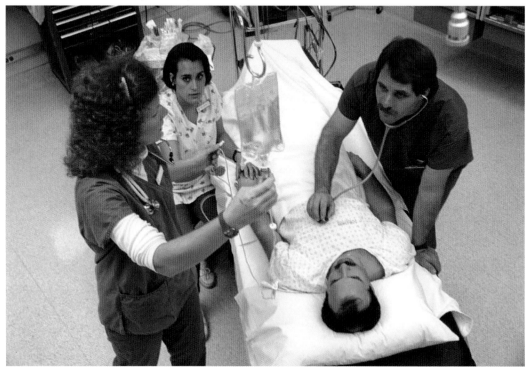

Trauma centers are usually located in big cities. Skilled teams are equipped to handle the most serious injuries. In trauma centers, there are always E.R. doctors available. They work regular 8- to 12-hour shifts. Those shifts may be at any time including nights, weekends, and holidays.

A trauma center is just one part of a large E.R., however. There are also parts that handle less critical conditions, such as broken bones or common illnesses. Many E.R.s have different sections for different levels of injuries. Some have special **pediatric** sections for younger patients.

The E.R. is often busy. Ringing phones, beeping pagers, and messages over the intercom sound throughout the E.R. There are always people darting around.

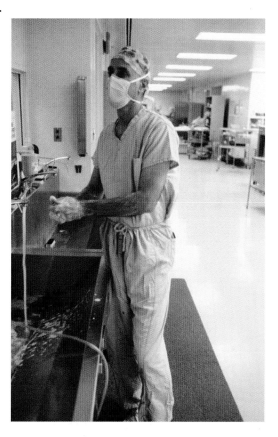

Doctors always wash their hands well before helping any patient.

There are doctors, nurses, and medical students. There are also technicians, patients, and worried family members. There are even police officers and **EMTs**.

People can arrive at the E.R. two ways. They can come on their own or by emergency **vehicle**. **Ambulances** and **helicopters** are emergency vehicles. Ambulances drop off patients at a special emergency door. Helicopters land near the E.R. or on the roof.

Sometimes, all the beds in a particular E.R. are full. Then, no more ambulances are allowed to come. Emergency vehicles must go to E.R.s that have available beds.

Everyone who comes to the E.R. must be checked in. The E.R. clerk does this. He or she writes important information about the patient and his or her condition. If the patient is not seriously ill, he or she provides that information. For serious injuries, the EMTs or other emergency workers may help.

Check-in information is relayed to the E.R. nurse. The nurse is the next person a noncritical patient will see. Nurses usually do the triage work. They determine who will be seen first. Most E.R. nurses are very experienced. They need to be familiar with a wide range of conditions.

After seeing the nurse, a patient may talk with an **intern** or a **resident**. Eventually, they will see an E.R. doctor. The doctor may send them to the lab. There, a technician may draw blood or take an X ray. These tests help the doctors determine what is wrong.

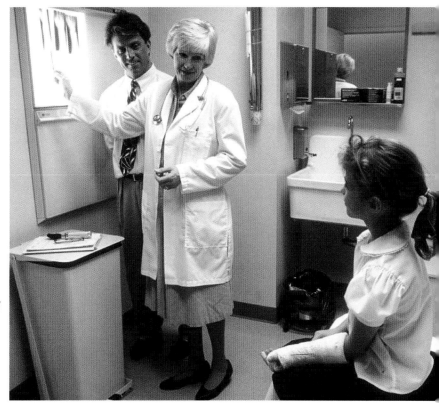

X rays and other tests help E.R. doctors determine what should be done to help an injury heal.

Help from Technology

Emergency medicine has improved greatly in recent years. New technology has led to many advances. Today, E.R. staff members have many tools to help them do their jobs.

Many people come to the E.R. with suspected heart attacks. E.R. doctors use an **electrocardiograph** to help **diagnose** these. The electrocardiograph creates a printout of the heart's activity. This helps doctors and nurses monitor the patient's heart.

Sometimes a person's heart starts beating irregularly. Doctors may then use a **defibrillator**. This machine shocks the heartbeat back into a normal rhythm.

X rays and other tests help E.R. doctors diagnose internal problems. These include broken bones, lung damage, or tumors.

Opposite page: These doctors are studying an electrocardiograph's printout to see how their patient's heart is working.

E.R. doctors also frequently order blood tests. The most common is called the complete blood count (CBC). A CBC counts red and white blood cells and platelets. This tells doctors how much blood a patient has lost. It can alert them to internal bleeding. Blood tests also tell doctors what blood type a patient has.

When to Seek Help

E.R. doctors like to teach people when to come to the E.R. It's a good idea to talk with your parents about when and how to call 911.

Call 911 if someone:
- Has stopped breathing or has no pulse
- Appears to be choking
- Has trouble breathing
- Is unconscious or won't wake up
- Is bleeding heavily
- Has suffered a bad head, neck, or back injury
- Has a possible broken or fractured bone
- Has a possible dislocated joint
- Has an eye injury
- Is in severe pain

Talking with your parents and other adults will help you be prepared in an emergency.

Glossary

ambulance - a vehicle that carries sick or injured people.

antibiotic - a substance used to kill bacteria or viruses.

asthma - a condition that makes breathing difficult and causes wheezing and coughing.

cardiopulmonary resuscitation - an emergency lifesaving method in which someone tries to restart a patient's heart and lungs. It is commonly called CPR.

chaos - a state of utter confusion.

civilian - a person who is not a member of the armed forces.

defibrillator - a tool used to restart or regulate a heartbeat.

diagnose - to find out by tests or examination.

electrocardiograph - an instrument used to see if the heart is working properly.

Emergency Medical Technician (EMT) - a person who is medically trained to assist patients at the scene of an emergency.

helicopter - an aircraft without wings that is lifted from the ground and kept in the air by horizontal propellers.

intern - an advanced student or graduate gaining supervised practical experience. A person doing this is participating in an internship.

Korean War - 1950 to 1953. A war between North and South Korea. The U.S. government sent troops to help South Korea.

mobile - easy to move.

pediatrics - a branch of medicine dealing with children.

prescribe - to order as medicine or treatment.

residency - a period of advanced training in a medical specialty after graduation from medical school and licensing to practice medicine. A person doing this is called a resident.

shock - a great weakening of the body that sometimes causes a person to become unconscious. Usually this is caused by blood loss.

specialize - to pursue one particular branch of study, called a specialty. A person who does this is a specialist.

transfusion - to transfer, as blood, into a vein of a person or animal.

trauma - a bodily wound or injury.

vehicle - any device used for carrying persons or objects.

World War II - 1939 to 1945, fought in Europe, Asia, and Africa. The United States, France, Great Britain, the Soviet Union, and their allies were on one side. Germany, Italy, Japan, and their allies were on the other side. The war began when Germany invaded Poland. The United States entered the war in 1941 after Japan bombed Pearl Harbor, Hawaii.

Web Sites

Would you like to learn more about your health and E.R. doctors? Please visit **www.abdopub.com** to find up-to-date Web site links that show you the history of doctors and fun ways to stay healthy. These links are routinely monitored and updated to provide the most current information available.

Index